THE PEARL OF PSALMS

THE PEARL OF PSALMS

PSALM XXIII

The Lord is my Shepherd, I shall not want.

He maketh me to lie down in green pastures : He leadeth me beside the still waters.

He restoreth my soul ; He leadeth me in the paths of righteousness for His name's sake.

Yea, though I walk through the valley of the shadow of death, I will fear no evil : for Thou art with me ; Thy rod and Thy staff they comfort me.

Thou preparest a table before me in the presence of mine enemies ; Thou anointest my head with oil ; my cup runneth over.

Surely goodness and mercy shall follow me all the days of my life : and I will dwell in the house of the Lord for ever.

THE PEARL OF PSALMS

by

GEORGE HENDERSON, F.R.G.S., M.R.S.L.

Author of
HEAVEN'S CURE FOR EARTH'S CARE
STUDIES IN THE BOOK OF EXODUS
etc., etc.

and as

" HENRY DURBANVILLE "

THE BEST IS YET TO BE
WINSOME CHRISTIANITY
HIS LAST WORDS
etc., etc.

Published by
B. McCALL BARBOUR
28 GEORGE IV BRIDGE
EDINBURGH, 1, SCOTLAND

Ninth Edition 1958
Tenth Edition 1966
Paperback Edition 1978

Reprinted 2001

© B. McCall Barbour

ISBN 0 7132 0029 4

Cover design and printing
Summit Media & Print Ltd
Old Kilpatrick G60 5JU UK

CONTENTS

PREFACE

DR. BARTON has said that the twenty-third is the sweetest of all the Psalms : first learned, oftenest repeated, longest remembered. The simple words of which it is composed " touch, inspire, comfort us, not as an echo from three thousand years ago, but as the voice of a living friend. The child repeats them at his mother's knees ; the scholar expends on them his choicest learning ; the Church lifts them to heaven in the many-voiced chorus. They fall like music on the sick man's ear and heart ; they cheer and encourage the dying Christian as he enters the shadow of death."

It speaks of the Shepherd Who gave His life for the sheep (verse 1) ; of the green pastures into which He leads us for our own sake (verse 2) ; and of the paths of righteousness into which He leads us for His name's sake (verse 3). It tells us that the valley of the shadow, although full of deadly peril, is nevertheless an avenue to God (verse 4) ; of the fact that it is possible to have festivity in the midst of conflict (verse 5) ; and of the two shining ones—Goodness and Mercy—who have come from the upper sanctuary to conduct the flock of God to the heavenly land (verse 6). In other words we have in this brief section of the Word : the Person (verse 1) ; the provision (verse 2) ; the pathway . (verse 3) ; the peril (verse 4) ; the preparation (verse 5) ; and the prospect (verse 6). May we all search more and more into its marvellous depths, enjoy increasingly its matchless beauty, and experience, through all life's future days, its perennial power.

In sending forth another edition of " The Pearl of Psalms ", I cannot refrain from expressing my gratitude to the One Who has deigned to use such a simple instrument to achieve such wonderful ends. May His blessing continue to rest upon it for His name's sake.

GEORGE HENDERSON.
(Henry Durbanville).

THE PEARL OF PSALMS

" They talk to me of music rare,
  Of anthems soft and low,
Of harps and viols, and angel choirs—
  All these I could forego;

" But the music of the Shepherd's voice,
  Which won my wayward heart,
Is the only strain I ever heard
  With which I cannot part."

INTRODUCTION

UNFOLDING as they do in the language of experience that which is laid down elsewhere doctrinally, the Psalms possess, for pilgrims heavenward, a peculiar charm. They record the experiences of a godly man in the midst of ungodliness, the aspirations of one who, although frequently baffled in his attempt to realize it, is possessed of an inextinguishable desire to live in fellowship with God ; and hence it is that to these Psalms the people of God in all ages have resorted, and from them have drawn that spiritual encouragement which they are eminently fitted to impart.

Chief among them is the beautiful twenty-third psalm. It is the most charming lyrical gem that has ever been penned, and has been compared to the nightingale and to the lark. It resembles the former of these songsters in that it sings most sweetly of all the psalms ; and the latter in that it *ascends* as it sings, directing us eventually to a place of perpetual song—" the House of the Lord ". It presents such a perfect union of unfaltering faith and

steadfast hope, of calm trustfulness and glad anticipation,
that one is not surprised to find in those who master it
and are mastered by it, the exhibition, in varying degrees,
of the gratitude which recognizes that " every perfect
gift is from above " (James 1. 17), and of the " love
which casteth out fear " (1 John 4. 18). Speaking of
Addison, with whom Psalm 23 was a great favourite, Lord
Macaulay says that the feeling which predominates in
all his devotional writings is *gratitude* ; and that on the
goodness displayed in the twenty-third psalm (to which
he ascribed all the happiness of his life), he relied in the
hour of death, and on the love that casteth out fear. It is
thus not without good reason that this portion of Scripture
has been called *the pearl of psalms*, just as Luke 15 has
been called *the pearl of parables*, and Isaiah 53 *the pearl
of prophecies*.

Before considering the Psalm itself in detail, we shall
glance at its setting ; for, like all other gems which are
appropriately set, the intrinsic lustre of this one is
enhanced when so viewed. Psalm 22 which precedes it
is the " Psalm of the Cross ". From it our Lord quoted
when, as the divinely-appointed Sin-bearer, He met the
grim realities of death and judgment—bearing the latter
and robbing the former of its sting (compare Psalm 22. 1 ;
Mark 15. 34). Passing into Psalm 23 we meet Him on the
resurrection side of the Cross. He has rent asunder the
fetters of the tomb, has risen a triumphant Conqueror
over death, and is now engaged in leading His sheep into
the green pastures and beside the still waters. In Psalm
24 we are pointed onwards to the time when He shall
sway the sceptre of universal righteousness—King of
kings and Lord of lords. Thus Psalm 22 depicts the
sufferings of Christ, and Psalm 24 the *glory* that was to
follow, while between them lies Psalm 23, which describes
the experiences of the Christian from the moment of his
apprehension of the one, until his entrance into the other.
" The Lord will give grace "—that is Psalm 22 ; " and

glory "—that is Psalm 24 ; " no good thing will He with-
hold from them that walk uprightly "—that is Psalm 23
(see Psalm 84. 11).   And so we have :

Psalm 22	Psalm 23	Psalm 24
Cross	Crook	Crown
Grace	Guidance	Glory
Sword	Staff	Sceptre
Provision	Protection	Prospect
Substitute	Shepherd	Sovereign
Yesterday	To-day	Forever

Chapter I

THE SHEPHERD OF THE SHEEP

" The Lord is my Shepherd " (verse 1)

IN the New Testament, Christ is presented as Shepherd in a three-fold aspect. As He contemplated His atoning work, and those for whom it was to be accomplished, He spoke of Himself as the " GOOD Shepherd " (John 10. 11) ; as He is brought again from the dead by the power of God, He is called the " GREAT Shepherd " (Hebrews 13. 20) ; and in connection with His second appearing when He will reward all service rendered to the sheep of His pasture, He is styled the " CHIEF Shepherd " (1 Peter 5. 4). These correspond to Psalms 22, 23 and 24.

I. THE GOOD SHEPHERD—DEATH. The reader will observe a wondrous contrast suggested here ; for while under the old economy the lamb died for the shepherd, under the new one, the Shepherd died for the lambs (compare Exodus 12 and John 10). While it is true that all we like sheep had gone astray and thus merited only wrath, still the sword awoke, not against us, but against the Shepherd—the Man Who was Jehovah's Fellow ; and by a lovely parable Christ makes known to us the joy which He has in the salvation of the lost (compare Isaiah 53. 6 ; Zechariah 13. 7 ; Matthew 26. 31 ; Acts 20. 28 ; Luke 15. 3-7). And while it is also true that " none of the ransomed ever shall know how deep were the waters the Saviour crossed ", yet, through grace, they all may know that the waters have been crossed, that the judgment has been borne, and that in consequence

> " Justice now withstands no more
> And mercy yields her boundless store ".

10

II. The Great Shepherd—Resurrection. Redemption accomplished, He is now alive for evermore, and so we would have our young Christian friends—especially them—observe what He says of them in the tenth chapter of John's Gospel (see particularly verses 27-29). In verse 27 He describes the two marks which distinguish all His sheep : the mark on the *ear*—they hear His voice ; and the mark on the *foot*—they follow Him. And then, in verse 28, He says : " I give unto them eternal life and they shall never perish, neither shall any man pluck them out of My hand ". What assurance and comfort do these soul-emancipating words impart ! They tell us that the mighty Hand, which brought the universe into being and guides the planets in their lonely way, upholds and sustains the feeblest lamb in the flock of Christ ; that

> " The very hand our sins had pierced
> Is now our guard and guide ".

Because eternal life is a gift, it can never be earned ; because it is the gift of God it can never be forfeited (compare Romans 6. 23 ; 11. 29 ; Ecclesiastes 3. 14). " The Lord is thy keeper "—we are " kept by the power of God " (Psalm 121. 5 ; 1 Peter 1. 5).

III. The Chief Shepherd—Glory (1 Peter 5. 2-4). This passage is one of many in the Word of God which mark the difference between *salvation* and *rewards*. An examination of these Scriptures reveals the fact that in order to obtain *salvation* we must look to Christ ; and that to secure *rewards* we must look to ourselves—our ways, our acts, our lives. " Look unto Me and be ye saved "—that epitomizes the passages which deal with the first theme (Isaiah 45. 22) ; " look to yourselves . . . that ye receive a full reward "—that summarizes those dealings with the second (2 John 8). Salvation is for those who are lost ; rewards are given for the faithful services of the saved. Salvation may be possessed here and now (John 3. 36) ; rewards will be dispensed at the coming of

the Lord (Revelation 22. 12). To make this subject
clear, we briefly tabulate side by side three of the gifts of
God with their corresponding rewards :

Gifts	Rewards
(1) Life (John 5. 24)	Crown of Life (Rev. 2. 10)
(2) Righteousness (2 Cor. 5. 21)	Crown of Righteousness (2 Tim. 4. 6-8)
(3) Glory (John 17. 22)	Crown of Glory (1 Peter 5. 4)

The message to the Christians at Smyrna was " be thou
faithful unto death and I will give thee "—not " life ",
for that they already possessed, but—" a crown of life ".
After a life of strenuous service for Christ, Paul could say
that there awaited him—not " righteousness ", for that
he already possessed, but " a crown of righteousness ".
And in the passage which we are now examining, the
apostle encourages the faithful under-shepherds of the
flock of God by reminding them that, when the Chief
Shepherd shall appear, they shall receive—not " glory ",
for that they would get by gift divine, but " a crown of
glory ". Of course, the hope of earning rewards should
not be the *motive* for service to Christ. They are, however, an incentive ; and God's purpose in promising them
is to win His people " from the pursuit of earthly riches
and pleasures, to sustain them in the fires of persecution,
and to encourage them in the exercise of Christian virtues".
   Such then, briefly, is the three-fold description of the
shepherd character of our Lord. He died to save ; He
lives to keep ; He is coming to reward. His death
secures our deliverance from the *penalty* of sin (1 Peter
2. 24) ; His intercession on high ensures our emancipa-
tion from the *power* of sin (Hebrews 7. 25) ; and at His
second coming He shall conduct us from the *presence* of
sin to fountains of living water, and reward His faithful
pastors with amaranthine crowns of glory, compared with
which the laurels that a Cæsar reaps are weeds(Revelation
7. 17, R.V.).

CHAPTER II

ABOUNDING PROVISION

" I shall not want " (verse 1)

THESE words are as firmly linked to the clause which precedes them, as consequence is to cause. With the Shepherd leading on in front of him, and " goodness and mercy ", like two faithful sheep-dogs, following hard behind him, David was as certain that he would not want anything here, as he was that he would dwell in the house of the Lord hereafter (compare John 10. 4 ; Psalm 23. 1 and 6).

Now, if for the moment we regard Psalm 23 as a sweet-toned instrument, and faith as the hand which plays upon it, we shall find that it yields to that touch, music of the most exquisite sweetness. What is it that " I shall not want "? The hand of faith runs over the key-board and brings out twelve distinct notes. Listen to them :

I shall not want REST,
    for He maketh me to lie down.
I shall not want REFRESHMENT,
    for He leads me by still waters.
I shall not want PRESERVATION,
    for He restoreth my soul.
I shall not want GUIDANCE,
    for He leadeth me.
I shall not want PEACE,
    for I will fear no evil.
I shall not want COMPANIONSHIP,
    for Thou art with me.

I shall not want COMFORT,
> for Thy rod and staff comfort me.

I shall not want SUSTENANCE,
> for Thou preparest a table.

I shall not want JOY,
> for Thou anointest my head.

I shall not want ANYTHING,
> for my cup runneth over.

I shall not want HAPPINESS now,
> for goodness and mercy follow me.

I shall not want GLORY hereafter,
> for I shall dwell in the house of
> the Lord forever.

The first of these notes—the only one upon which we have space to dwell—is drawn out and interpreted for us by the Master Himself in Matthew 11. 28-30 : " Come unto Me, all ye that labour and are heavy laden, and I will give you rest. Take My yoke upon you, and learn of Me ; for I am meek and lowly in heart : and ye shall find rest unto your souls. For My yoke is easy and My burden is light."

In that wonderful story *Uncle Tom's Cabin*, one of the characters is represented as being at the bedside of a dying negress, whom he seeks to comfort by the Word of God. In the course of his ministrations he quoted the words of the Saviour : " Come unto Me, . . . and I will give you rest ", and by so doing immediately arrested the attention of the dying woman. " Them is good words," she said, " who speaks them ? " Ah, that is the point upon which their value depends—" who speaks them ? " Spoken by any other, these words would only tantalize ; spoken by the Lord Jesus Christ, they can banish a world of sorrow and unrest, and establish a universe of bliss. Behind them is the claim, on the part of the Speaker, of ability to more than counterbalance the woes of sinning and suffering humanity; and the testimony of the centuries goes to demonstrate unequivocally the validity of that claim. On hearts that once were restless as the troubled sea they have fallen like the quiet dew from heaven, stilling the fever in blood and brain, and exchanging for the unrest of sin " the unutterable joy of shadowless communion " (compare Isaiah 57. 20, 21 ; Philippians 4. 6, 7).

These verses tell us of something to *do*—" come " ; of something to *leave*—our " burden " ; of something to *take*—" My yoke " ; and of something to *find*—" rest ". In order to understand the significance of the whole passage, however, we must notice that it speaks of two kinds of rest—one in verse 28, and one in verse 29. The first of these is a gift—" I will *give* you rest " ; the second is a discovery—" ye shall *find* rest ". The one is the rest of *salvation* ; the other is the rest of *sanctification*. The former—rest of *conscience*—is unconditional, being imparted by Christ to all who, in response to His invitation, come to Him ; the latter—rest of *heart*—is conditional upon our learning of Him, Who is meek and lowly of heart.

Meekness and lowliness : these represent the active and the passive sides of humility—a virtue which, because of its rarity, commands universal esteem.

> " The bird that soars on highest wing,
>   Builds on the ground her lowly nest,
> And she that doth most sweetly sing,
>   Sings in the shade when all things rest ;
> In lark and nightingale we see
>   What honour hath humility."

When walking in lowliness we are not likely to wound other people, and when walking in meekness we shall not allow ourselves to be offended should they happen to treat us in an unseemly manner. Is it not just the absence of these graces that causes so much fevered restlessness in our lives ? We want to do the work of the man with ten talents when God has gifted us with only one ; to occupy a prominent position in public when He intends us to fill a lowly place in private. Let us never forget that " when God intends a creature to fly He always provides it with wings " ; that if He has fitted one for publicity and prominence, the gift with which He has endowed that one will inevitably make room for itself (Proverbs 18. 16). And the strong probability is that, did we but know the perils which surround those who occupy high positions and the fierce conflict which those have to wage who lead the van in Christian warfare, we would cease envying them and commence praying for them, and be thankful and content that we are filling, in lowly obscurity, the niche which God intends us to fill.

> " . . . As the storm that makes
> The high elm crouch and rends the oak
> The humble lily spares—so, a thousand blows
> That shake the lofty monarch on his throne
> We lesser folk feel not.   Keen are the pains
> Advancement often brings.   To be secure
> Be humble ; to be happy be content."

We follow on to think of His yoke and His burden. " My yoke," He says, " is easy ".   Let us consider what a yoke is really for.   Is it to be a burden to the animal which wears it ?   Surely not.   It is just the very opposite.   It is to make its labour light.   The plough, attached to the oxen in any other way than by a yoke, would make the work of ploughing intolerable.   By means of a yoke, it is light.   A yoke is not an instrument of torture ; it is an instrument of mercy.   It is not a malicious contrivance for making work hard ; it is a simple device to make hard labour light ; and the Saviour's yoke never chafes, for, as has been said, it is padded with meekness and lowliness of heart.   And then His burden is light.   It is such a burden as the wings are to a bird, or as the sails are to a boat.

Here, then, is the two-fold secret of rest.   Responding

to the Saviour's invitation, we find that the restlessness of the troubled sea gives place to the peace which flows like a river ; and by taking His yoke and learning of Him Who is meek and lowly in heart, we anticipate, and experience even now, the deep rest of heart that remains for the people of God (Hebrews 4. 9). Then, indeed, do we lie down in green pastures—satisfied.

> " O patient, spotless One,
>   Our hearts in meekness train
> To bear Thy yoke and learn of Thee,
>   That we may rest obtain."

Chapter III

SUSTENANCE AND REFRESHMENT

*" He maketh me to lie down in green pastures ; He leadeth
me beside the still waters "* (verse 2)

WE recall that, when the Israelites were passing
through the wilderness Canaan-wards, there were
two things which never failed them, viz., the *manna*,
and the *water*. The former was for their sustenance and
the latter for their refreshment ; and during that long
period of forty years each recurring day brought its
abundant supply (compare Psalm 78. 24 and Isa. 43. 20).
For the *spiritual* meaning of the manna compare Exodus
16 with John 6 ; and for that of the water compare
Exodus 17 with John 7.

Since the *wilderness* through which the Israelites passed
to their inheritance represents the *valley* experiences
through which we pass to ours, that two-fold provision
aptly sets forth the nourishment and refreshment which
form the theme of this chapter. The green pastures
sustain, the still waters *refresh* ; and our responsibility to
avail ourselves of them arises from the fact that, like the
manna and the *water*, they are freely provided. Each
morning, and with unfailing regularity, the soft showers
of *angels' food* reached the place of their sojourning (Psalm
78. 25) ; all they had to do was to gather, to appropriate,
and to enjoy, the full and ample provision for their needs
(Exodus 16. 14, 15). The manna was white—telling of
its purity (compare Exodus 16. 31 with Psalm 119. 140) ;
it tasted like honey—telling of its sweetness (compare
Exodus 16. 31 with Psalm 119. 103). When the people
departed from God, however, and returned in heart to
the land from which His outstretched arm had delivered
them, the manna lost its sweetness : they first made light

of it, and eventually despised it. " We remember the fish which we did eat in Egypt freely ; . . . but now our soul is dried away : there is nothing at all beside this manna, before our eyes." " Our soul loatheth this light bread " (compare Numbers 11. 5, 6 and 21. 5).

The lessons for us here are as obvious as they are valuable. The *manna* for the heavenly pilgrim of to-day —that which is to sustain him through all the vicissitudes of his career—is *Christ as presented in the Word of God by the power of the Spirit.* " Then said Jesus unto them, . . . My Father giveth you the true bread from heaven. For the bread of God is He which cometh down from heaven, and giveth life unto the world . . . I am the Bread of Life " (John 6. 32-35). But there is contrast as well as comparison in John 6 ; for while the manna was the perishable food of a transient life, He is the imperishable food of an endless life. " Your fathers did eat manna in the wilderness and are dead ; . . . if any man eat of *this* bread he shall live for ever " (verses 49 and 51). And since, as we have said, it is by means of the written Word that we feed on the living Word, we find Peter declaring that the Word of God by which the new life was first imparted is also the food by which it is sustained. " Being born again by the Word of God . . . as new-born babes desire the sincere milk of the Word that ye may grow thereby."

Of the manna, we read that " they gathered it every morning " (Exodus 16. 21). Viewed typically and spiritually, these words present a philosophy of life for the Christian believer. They constitute the secret of safety, of certainty, and of enjoyment. To the holy habit of daily feeding on the heavenly manna, which is set before us in the sacred page of Scripture, is attributable our joy (see Jeremiah 15. 16), our peace (Psalm 119. 165), our fruitfulness (Psalm 1. 2, 3), our security in the hour of peril (Psalm 17. 4). " Christian men and women must read and study the Word of God. No pressure of Chris-

tian work, in all the manifold activities of the present day,
should prevent the daily, devotional perusal of God's
Holy Word.   Christian effort cannot be substituted for
thoughtful and serious attention to what we are taught of
God in His holy Book, and by which we are to be renewed
and sanctified.   We must be filled with divine truth if we
are to grow in the divine life.   Our Christian activities,
furthermore, can only be sustained and enlarged by much
communion with Christ through His Word.   The sources
of great rivers are hidden away in mountain and glen.
Fountains burst out in secluded places, and gentle brooks
run through shaded ravines.   They meet at length, and,
mingling in their onward flow, set at work industrial
activity in a thousand shapes and forms.   But what would
keep all these activities in motion if the fountains should
fail, and the brooks be dried up ?   What shall sustain
steadily the long-continued effort of the Church of Christ
to overcome the world, the flesh, and the devil, save the
feeding of each member of the elect body in the green
pastures of the divine Word ?   The real power to do great
things for Christ must come from secluded places, where
men commune with God and gather motives, convictions
and incitements to effort, from His Word."   Let us remember, too, in this connection, to range over the whole
garden of Scripture and not to confine ourselves to a few
particularly wealthy spots ; for the green pastures are
everywhere.   By the anointed eye, Christ is as really
beheld in the types of the Pentateuch as in the later
portions of the inspired Word.   He is *enfolded* in the Old
Testament and *unfolded* in the New.   " Search the Scriptures," said He, " for they are they which testify of Me ".
" Had ye believed Moses ye would have believed Me ; for
he wrote of Me " (John 5. 39, 46).   And after His resurrection He joined the two disconsolate ones on their way
to Emmaus, and, " beginning at Moses and all the pro-
phets, He expounded unto them in *all* the Scriptures *the
things concerning Himself* " (Luke 24. 27).

> " Oh, what a Bible-reading have we here,
>   Not barren theory—musty, dry and drear—
>   But Christ, the ' altogether lovely ', full in view,
>   Himself the preacher, text and sermon too."

And thus we learn that if our souls are to be kept healthy,
vigorous, and strong ; that if our work for God is to be
of an enduring character ; that if we are to combat
successfully the principalities and powers which are
arrayed against us and which are determined to resist
every advance we attempt to make in the knowledge of
God—we *must* read and study the Word of God.

> " House of treasure ! here I find
>   Food and medicine for the mind,
>   Sword to wield against the foe,
>   Helm and shield to ward his blow,
>   Garments for the heavenly born,
>   Gems the spirit to adorn,
>   Songs of praise in sunny hours,
>   Dirges when the tempest lowers—
>   But I need not thus go on
>   Naming treasures one by one ;
>   Why should I the rest recall,
>   Christ is here, and Christ is all."

Let us just add, on the other hand, that to the neglect
of that Word can be traced joylessness, powerlessness, sin,
failure, spiritual disaster.   On one of the pages of the
Bible belonging to a young friend, these words are written:
" This Book will keep me from sin, or sin will keep me
from this Book ".   The statement is profoundly true.
Love for both can no more co-exist than ice under a
tropical sun, or darkness with light.

But there was not only *manna*, there was *water* from
the smitten rock, just as for us there are not only green
pastures to sustain, but also still waters to refresh.   That
rock is Christ (1 Corinthians 10. 4), Who has said, " the
water that I shall give him shall be in him a well of water
springing up into everlasting life " (John 4. 14).   *There*
is perennial refreshment.

There is, however, still deeper thought in the words of
our text ; for the point emphasized is not merely that the
green pastures are provided, but that He makes us to *lie
down* in them.   Now, a sheep never does that until it is
satisfied ;   and hence the spiritual significance of the
expression is complete satisfaction, absolute repose.   In
our early days of Christian experience we " mount up "
with wings as eagles, and heavenly things are very real ;
after a little while we learn that if we are in heaven as a
matter of *faith*, we are still in the midst of the stern
realities of life as a matter of *fact*, and we commence to
" run " with patience the race set before us.   By and
by we settle down, like Enoch, to the steady " walk "
with God ; and learn, like Mary, the value of " sitting "
at His feet to learn His Word.   And finally, we enter into
the experience of which our psalm speaks—we " lie
down " in green pastures—satisfied (compare Isaiah
40. 31 ; Hebrew 12. 1 ; Genesis 5. 24 ; Luke 10. 39 ;
Psalm 23. 2 ; Psalm 107. 9).

This is what men are wearily searching for, and this is
what, so long as they seek it at the broken cisterns of
earth, they will never find.   " Thou hast made us for
Thyself, O Lord, and we are restless till we rest in Thee."
So said Augustine ; and the truth of the statement has
been verified by men in all ages and in all climes.   One,
who drained the cup of earthly pleasure to its very dregs,
mournfully confessed that,

> " Although gay companions o'er the bowl
>   Dispel awhile the sense of ill ;
> Though pleasures fill the maddening soul,
>   The heart, the heart is lonely still ".

Another, who found repose for heart and conscience in
the person and work of the Redeemer, joyfully exclaimed,

> " I have heard the voice of Jesus,
>   Tell me naught of else beside ;
> I have seen the face of Jesus,
>   And my soul is satisfied ".

The Scriptures confirm these negative and positive testimonies by declaring that, while the pleasures of sin are transient, the pleasures which are at God's right hand are eternal (Hebrews 11. 25 ; Psalm 16. 11). Thus, three thoughts have been before us, namely, He feeds, He leads, and He satisfies. " He shall *feed* His flock like a shepherd " (Isaiah 40. 11) ; " He *leadeth* me beside the still waters " (Psalm 23. 2) ; " He *satisfieth* the longing soul " (Psalm 107. 9).

Here, then, is the provision which has been made for us by the great Shepherd under Whose care we now are. And by comparing Luke 15. 5 with Isaiah 40. 11, we learn that His strength and affection, His power and His love, are engaged on our behalf. He carries the sheep on His shoulders and the lambs in His bosom. May we all trust His power more artlessly, enjoy His love more constantly, and follow Himself more faithfully.

CHAPTER IV

DIVINE RESTORATION
" He restoreth my soul " (verse 3)

THESE words are as solemn as they are blessèd. They
are solemn because they suggest, even as David's per-
sonal history illustrates, that the best of us may, if unwatchful, fall into sin ; and they are blessèd because they remind
us that, although a good man may fall, he shall rise
again ; that although a Christian may cause clouds to
come between himself and his Lord, and forfeit the joy of
the relationship in which through grace he stands, God,
in the exercise of His sovereign grace, can intervene to
scatter those clouds and restore that joy (compare Psalms
37 and 51).

This verse, indeed, suggests solemn possibilities ; for
surely there can be no more solemn possibility than that
of wandering from God, whether it be in heart or in
conduct. Among the many evils attendant upon such
an unhappy course is this one, namely, every moment so
spent is lost time. In illustration of what we mean may
we turn to the eleventh chapter of Hebrews. That
chapter—the Westminster Abbey of the Bible, as it has
been called—contains the epitaphs inscribed upon the
tombstones of God's heroes, and in fulfilment of Hebrews
10. 17, he omits their failures and records only their
victories. In verse 29 we read that " by faith the
Israelites passed through the Red Sea as by dry land " ;
and in the next verse that " by faith the walls of Jericho
fell down after they were compassed about seven days ".
But between these two events there was a period of forty
years—a period which, alas, Israel spent in wilfulness and
in wandering. One may ask, " What about that ? "
Well, it is not mentioned just because it was failure and
therefore was lost time.

24

On a sun-dial in a certain churchyard these words are written : " I number none but the cloudless hours ". The years which Israel spent in wilderness wandering were indeed dark and overcast with heavy clouds ; and for that reason they are unnumbered, uncounted. During that period they were like a regiment of soldiers marking time, or like a man, who, having lost his way, spends a great deal of his time in getting right again. And Israel's history at this juncture reminds us of another solemn principle in the governmental dealings of God, namely, that one who has gone astray will get right exactly *at the spot where he went wrong*. It was at Kadesh-barnea that they listened to the unbelieving spies and began to wander ; it was from that same spot, nearly forty years afterwards, that they commenced the forward march which culminated in their entrance into, and conquest of, the land of Canaan (compare Numbers 13 ; Deuteronomy 1. 19-22 ; 2. 14).

In the restoration of those who, by reason of sin or indifference, wander from Him, God employs two things, namely, His *voice*, and His *hand* ; His *word* and His *chastisement*. Let us meditate on these for a moment.

I. RESTORATION BY THE WORD. There is a scene in the life of the Apostle Peter which beautifully illustrates this. The sifting process of which our Lord had warned him, but to which he paid little attention, had been carried out ; and as a result Peter had denied his Master with oaths and curses. One can imagine the remorse which would fill his mind when he realized what he had done : the tendency would be to throw up utterly his new discipleship. And here we would point out the meaning of a Scripture which is frequently misquoted. Our Lord had said, " I have prayed for thee that *thy faith* fail not," not " that *thou* mayest fail not ". The failure was evidently the only method by which Peter could be robbed of his self-confidence. But the danger was that, having fallen, he would give way to despair, and it was to obviate this that our Lord's intercession was exercised on his behalf. Well, just at the time of Peter's great denial, " the Lord turned, and looked upon Peter. And Peter remembered the *word* of the Lord, how He had said unto him, ' before the cock crow, thou shalt deny Me thrice '. And Peter went out and wept bitterly " (Luke 22. 61, 62). " Peter called to mind the word that Jesus said unto him . . . and when he thought thereon, he wept " (Mark 14. 72). That word penetrated Peter's soul, broke up the fountains of his heart, and drew forth floods of penitential tears. " When he meant his best he found out what a wicked heart he had ; and when he did his worst he found out what a blessèd heart Christ had."

How oft in times of soul declension do we experience equally tender treatment from our gracious God ! " Return, thou backsliding Israel, and I will not cause Mine anger to fall upon you ; return, ye backsliding children, and I will heal your backsliding "—*there* is the *voice* of love divine seeking to arrest the declension, to woo the the wanderer from the error of his way, and by so doing to spare him the necessity of feeling the weight of the divine *hand* (Jeremiah 3. 12, 22 ; Hosea 14). If, however, that voice is disregarded, and the wrong course persisted in, the only alternative is—

II. RESTORATION BY CHASTISEMENT. Chastisement is one of our unpleasant blessings. In the exercise of it God reveals " the graver countenance of love ". Correctly to understand its purpose and meaning and value, however, we must remember that it is not always or necessarily the result of sin. It is quite true, as the history of the ages solemnly testifies, that " whatsoever a man soweth, that shall he also reap " (Galatians 6. 7) ; that, as one of our poets expresses it,

" . . . Sorrow follows wrong, as echo follows song,
    And every guilty deed holds within itself the seed
        Of retribution and undying pain ".

But, admitting all this, the fact remains that retribution does not exhaust the purposes of God in chastisement. He has also lessons of education and soul-culture to teach by its means—lessons which, when learned, will issue in " the peaceable fruit of righteousness unto them which are exercised thereby " (Hebrews 12. 11). It is for this reason that we are exhorted to " despise not the chastening of the Lord ; neither be weary of His correction : for whom the Lord loveth He correcteth, even as a father the son in whom he delighteth " (Proverbs 3. 11, 12).

Assured, then, that chastisement may be educative as well as retributive, and that in either case it is the evidence of a love which ever has our profit in view, we turn to consider the classic passage which deals with it— Hebrews 12. 5-11. And if we examine that passage carefully we find that chastisement has always one of three effects upon us ; we either *despise* it, or *faint* under it, or *are exercised* by it.

(1) *Despising it* (v. 5). The famous oriental philosopher, Lokman, while a slave, being presented by his master with a bitter melon, immediately ate it all. " How was it possible," said his master, " for you to eat so nauseous a fruit ? " Lokman replied, " I have received so many favours from you, it is no wonder I should, for once in my life, eat a bitter melon from your hand ". The generous answer of the slave struck the master so forcibly, that he immediately gave him his liberty. Unlike Lokman's master, however, our God never chastens arbitrarily or unnecessarily. He always chastens for our profit (v. 10) ; and the recognition of that grand fact will act as a mighty deterrent in the soul that is in danger of " despising the chastening of the Lord ". Then there is the danger of

(2) *Fainting under it* (v. 5). Those of us who have examined coal trucks on the railway have noticed that each is endorsed with its carrying capacity : one " To carry 12 tons ", another, " To carry 20 tons ", and so on.

The builder of these trucks knows their frame and pre-
scribes exactly how much weight they are to carry.   And
He Who " knoweth *our* frame " (Psalm 103. 14) never
suffers us to be tested above what we are able to bear
(1 Corinthians 10. 13), but, as occasion necessitates,
gives power to the faint and to those that have no might
increase of strength (Isaiah 40. 29), so that as our days
so shall our strength be (Deuteronomy 33. 25).   If we
despise the chastening of the Lord or faint when we are
rebuked of Him, we lose the blessing which He intends to
send us by these means.   Chastisement yields its peaceable fruits only to those who are

(3) *Exercised by it* (v. 11).   We read of a Christian
blacksmith who had a good deal of affliction, and who was
challenged by an unbeliever to account for it.   This was
his explanation : " I don't know that I can account for
these things to *your* satisfaction, but I think I can to
my *own*.   You know that I am a blacksmith.   I often
take a piece of iron, and put it in the fire, and bring it to a
white heat.   Then I put it on the anvil, and strike it once
or twice to see if it will take a temper.   If I think it will,
I plunge it into the water, and suddenly change its tem-
perature.   Then I put it into the fire again, and again I
I plunge it into the water.   This I repeat several times.
Then I put it on the anvil, and hammer it into some
useful article which I put into a carriage, where it does
good service for twenty-five years.   If, however, when
I first strike it on the anvil, I think it will not take a
temper, I throw it into the scrap heap, and sell it as
scrap metal.   Now, I believe that my heavenly Father
has been testing me to see if I would take a temper.   He
has put me into the fire and put me into the water.   I
have tried to bear it as patiently as I could, and my daily
prayer has been, ' Lord, put me into the fire if you think
I do need it ; do anything you please, O Lord, only, for
Christ's sake, don't throw me into the scrap heap '."

Another Christian man who was similarly afflicted has

said : " The file is rough, and the application of it harrowing to the soul ; but all the brighter and more lustrous will be the diamond, when, at length, thoroughly polished, it shines forth in the royal crown of Emmanuel ".

> " In the still air the music lies unheard,
>   In the rough marble beauty hides unseen,
> To wake the music and the beauty needs
>   The master's touch, the sculptor's chisel keen.
> Great Master, touch us with Thy skilful hand,
>   Let not the music that is in us die,
> Great Sculptor, hew and polish us, nor let,
>   Hidden and lost, Thy form within us lie."

To prevent misconception regarding the purpose of chastisement, we have dealt with it in this chapter in a general way ; but the application of that part of it which bears on our immediate theme is simple and easy. Is it the case that " the consolations of God are small with thee " (Job 15. 11)? If so, is there not a cause for this ? Let conscience cast her enlightened gaze over the past, and she will probably lead thee to the very moment when the current of peace ceased to flow ; when the stream of joy became interrupted. Oh, that thou hadst hearkened to His commandments ! Then had thy peace been as a river, and thy righteousness as the waves of the sea (Isaiah 48. 18). If, however, we have failed to listen to His voice, then it is needful to make absolutely certain that we " hear the rod and recognize Who hath appointed it " (Micah 6. 9). His purpose in it all is to restore us to Himself ; and, although the process may be a painful one, the end is blessed. " If we confess our sins, He is faithful and just to forgive us our sins, and to cleanse us from all unrighteousness " (1 John 1. 9). " No chastening for the present seemeth to be joyous, but grievous ; nevertheless afterward it yieldeth the peaceable fruit of righteousness unto them which are exercised thereby " (Hebrews 12. 11).

CHAPTER V

THE UNERRING GUIDE

" He leadeth me in the paths of righteousness for His name's sake " (verse 3)

" HEART sorrow and a clear life ensuing." This quotation from Shakespeare, although not intended by him to form a definition of repentance, does, nevertheless, form an almost perfect one. It links the theme of this chapter with that of the last. " He restoreth my soul "—why? He does so in order that He may " lead me in the paths of righteousness for His name's sake ".

It will generally be found that the Christian who has wandered from God, and learned the bitterness of " sowing to the flesh ", becomes, after restoration—which implies repentance—a more careful and a more prayerful person than ever before. " Before I was afflicted, I went astray ; but now have I kept Thy Word " (Psalm 119. 67). " It is good for me that I have been afflicted, that I might learn Thy statutes " (Psalm 119. 71, 75). Think of Peter. His bitter tears evidenced his " heart sorrow " ; his subsequent history demonstrates the " clear life ". The erstwhile braggart has become a humble, broken man ; and, instead of self-confident boasting, he manifests a spirit at once calm, mellowed, and subdued. He exemplifies the truth of Tennyson's word which declares that

> " Men may rise on stepping-stones
> Of their dead selves to higher things ".

I. HE LEADETH ME IN THE PATHS OF RIGHTEOUSNESS. Turning to the New Testament for an interpretation of this phrase, we find it in Titus 2. 12. That verse is the central one of three which, together, form an epitome of the whole of the New Testament Scriptures. The eleventh verse epitomizes the gospels ; the twelfth verse summarizes the epistles ; and the thirteenth, the book of Revelation. The first of these verses unfolds a salvation which is as full as it is free ; the second teaches lessons which are as valuable as they are complete ; while the third presents a hope which triumphs over death, and exults in the vision of immortality. Between the reception of the Gospel as set forth in verse 11, and the fulfilment of the blessèd hope spoken of in verse 13, we are to tread the " paths of righteousness " set before us in verse 12 : we are to " deny ungodliness and wordly lusts, and live sobermindedly, righteously, and godly, in this present world ". And since His ways are ways of pleasantness and all His paths are peace, we may safely assert that the believer who learns these lessons thoroughly will have a peace as deep as the sea, and as still as the stars.

Regarding the lessons themselves, we would observe that these are of a two-fold character—negative and positive; and that the negative lessons come first, teaching us to deny ourselves " ungodliness and worldly lusts ". This is ever the divine order : we must " cease to do evil " before we can " learn to do well " (Isaiah 1. 16, 17) ; we must " abhor that which is evil " before we can " cleave to that which is good " (Romans 12. 9). Is there not an explanation here of the meagreness of our growth in grace ? We do well to " desire the sincere milk of the Word that we may grow thereby " (1 Peter 2. 2) ; but an indispensable pre-requisite to growth in grace is the " laying aside of all malice, and all guile, and hypocrisies, and envies, and all evil speakings " (1 Peter 2. 1). How searching is the truth of God !

But there is a second standard in the school of grace ; a standard in which positive lessons are taught ; in which we learn to live " sobermindedly, righteously, and godly, in this present world ". Let us observe carefully these three great words—sobermindedly, righteously, and

godly—they embrace everything. " Sobermindedly "—
that has reference to the world *within*. Our thoughts,
our tongues, our tempers, are to be held in complete
subjection ; and the body, no longer the slave of sin, is
to become the vehicle for the accomplishment of the
will of God. " Righteously "—that has reference to the
world *without*. We are to manifest *practically* in the world
what we are *judicially* in the eyes of Heaven. " Godly "
—that refers to the world *above*. " If ye then be risen
with Christ, seek those things which are above, where
Christ sitteth on the right hand of God " (Colossians
3. 1 ; Psalm 4. 3). Connected with the learning of the
first of these positive lessons we read that " he that is slow
to anger is better than the mighty ; and he that ruleth
his spirit than he that taketh a city " (Proverbs 16. 32) ;
connected with the second, is the possession of " a
conscience void of offence toward God and *men* " (Acts
24. 16) ; while the student who learns the third, enters
into the deep, glad consciousness of life and peace : " to
be spiritually-minded is life and peace " (Romans 8. 6).
We have the safest of guide books to direct us in these
paths of righteousness (Psalm 119. 105) ; and the most
patient of teachers to teach us those lessons (Job 36. 22).
Let us see that in all our ways we acknowledge Him,
assured as we are that He can and will direct our paths
(Proverbs 3. 6).

II. FOR HIS NAME'S SAKE. If the second clause
tells us *where* He leads, this last clause points out *why*
He leads us there. " He leadeth me in the paths of
righteousness "—not that a reputation for saintliness may
be won ; nor that any man may be able to say to his
fellows, " stand by thyself for I am holier than thou " ;
but—" *for His name's sake* ". God has connected His
name and glory with the walk and conduct of His people
on earth ; and the solemn obligation is laid upon " every
one that nameth the name of Christ to depart from ini-
quity " (2 Timothy 2. 19). Nor is our testimony to be

merely a negative one : there must be not only abstinence from every form of evil, but the positive setting forth by life and by lip, in speech and in action, of the fragrance of that Name which is as " ointment poured forth " (Song of Solomon 1. 3). " The name of Jesus," says one, ". . . is a summing up of the hallelujahs of eternity in five letters ".

It has been decreed that, in a coming day, every knee shall bow to that Name (Philippians 2. 9, 10). Happy are they who, constrained by His love, bow to and acknowledge it now ; for by yielding themselves to Him they antedate, in the experience of their lives, that glad time, so frequently spoken of by seer and prophet, when the kingdoms of this world shall have become the kingdoms of our Lord and of His Christ (Revelation 11. 15).

> " Many friends are near, but He is nearest,
>   Always what we want, and all our own.
> Many names are dear, but His is dearest,
>   How it grows more dear as life goes on !
>   Jesus, Jesus ! let us ever say it
>   Softly to ourselves as some sweet spell.
>   Jesus, Jesus ! troubled spirit lay it
>   On thy heart, and it will make thee well."

CHAPTER VI

PROVISION FOR THE VALLEY

" Yea, though I walk through the valley of the shadow of death, I will fear no evil ; for Thou art with me ; Thy rod and Thy staff they comfort me " (verse 4)

IF Psalm 23 is one of the most precious portions of the Word of God, the verse which heads this chapter is perhaps the most precious portion of that psalm. It voices the confidence which has marked the career and closing hours on earth of myriads of the saints of God ; it shall continue to do so until the one flock and the one Shepherd shall have passed to the ever verdant fields and the everlasting hills, where there are no dangers to alarm and no foes to affright (compare John 10. 16 R.V. ; Revelation 7. 17 R.V.).

This Scripture has a two-fold message. It has a message of peace for the heavenly pilgrim who is nearing life's close, and it has a message of power for the one before whom life lies as an untrodden path. Let us glance at these in the order named.

I. THE MESSAGE OF PEACE. One of the most pathetic utterances to be found within the whole range of English literature is that of the aged chieftain, who, urging upon his king the reception of the first missionaries to England said—" So seems the life of man, O King ! as a sparrow's flight through the hall when a man is sitting at meat in winter-tide, with the warm fire lighted on the hearth but the chill rain-storm without. The sparrow flies in at one door, tarries for a moment in the light and heat of the hearth fire, and then flying forth from the other, vanishes into the wintry darkness whence it came. So tarries for a moment the life of man in our sight ; but what is before it, what after it, we know not. If this new teaching tell us aught certainly of these, let us follow it."

Apart from the light which divine revelation sheds on the past and on the future, man is an enigma to himself : he knows not whence he has come, nor whither he is going. And because of this, there has always been what the greatest of our poets calls an instinctive " dread of something after death ". We read in Hebrews 2. 15, of those " who through fear of death were all their lifetime subject to bondage " ; and Shakespeare says that " he that cuts off twenty years of life cuts off so many years of fearing death ". Standing, however, as we now are, under the meridian ray of the full-orbed gospel, and possessing, as we now do, the clear light and sure word of Him Who has abolished death, and brought life and immortality to light through the gospel, there is, for the Christian believer, no need for uncertainty, no need for alarm (compare Hebrews 2. 14 ; 2 Timothy 1. 10 ; 1 Corinthians 15. 55). The gospel robs life of its bitterness, and death of its sting : indeed death is now numbered among the things which are said to be " yours " (1 Corinthians 3. 21-23).

In the four New Testament passages which deal with the passing of the ransomed spirit from this world, there is a wealth of instruction and comfort. We shall merely touch on them. Luke 23. 39-43, which is the first of them, illustrates how our Lord does " exceeding abundantly above all that we ask or think ". The penitent thief had prayed " Lord, remember me when Thou comest into Thy kingdom ", which prayer, had it been answered literally, would have meant two millenniums of separation from the Saviour's immediate presence. The Saviour's answer, however, was : " Verily I say unto thee, *to-day* shalt thou be with Me *in paradise* ". The second passage is Acts 7. 59-60. Here we have the first of that noble army of men and women who " lived unknown till persecution dragged them into fame and

chased them up to Heaven ". Although, as Tennyson
points out in his fine eulogy, Stephen was cursed and
scorned and bruised with stones, he prayed for his
murderers ; and, having done that, his poor battered
body sank to rest—" he fell asleep ". The third passage
is 2 Corinthians 5. 1-8. The contrast there, so far as our
theme is concerned, is between " the earthly house of
this tabernacle " and " the house not made with hands,
eternal in the heavens " (verse 1). " Yours is a frail
tabernacle," said someone to an invalid Christian.
" Yes," was the reply, " but I have a magnificent view
from it ". We nightly pitch that tent a day's march
nearer Home ; and when it is struck for the last time, we
shall be absent from the body and present with the Lord
(verse 8). The fourth passage is Philippians 1. 21-24.
The apostle is in a dilemma. On the one hand, he yearns
to depart and be with Christ which is far, far better (verse
23). On the other hand, he recognizes that his divinely
imparted gifts were greatly needed by his brethren in
Christ. Unselfish love wins the day. He is willing to
forego what would be his own supreme joy, for their
furtherance and joy of faith (verse 25).

If we examine these passages carefully, all fear of death
will be swept from us as the thistledown is swept before
the hurricane ; it will vanish as do the mists before the
rising sun. For the believer

> " There is no death ! What seems so is transition ;
>   This life of mortal breath
> Is but a suburb of the life Elysian,
>   Whose portal we call death."

If we lay hold of this fact once for all, then, notwith-
standing the relative solemnities of life and death, we will
be constrained to pray : " Teach me to *live*, 'tis easier
far to die ".

II. THE MESSAGE OF POWER. But if Psalm 23, verse 4
affords comfort to the Christian whose course is almost

run, it does infinitely more to the one who is at the starting point. We would observe that it is "the *shadow* of death" that is spoken of ; and, comparing Isaiah 9. 2 with Luke 1. 76-79, it will be found that that expression is significant of *this world*. As we saw in the Introduction, Psalm 22 is the "hill of Calvary" (see verse 1), and Psalm 24, "the hill of the Lord" (see verse 3) ; and "the valley of the shadow of death" represents those darker, more trying experiences through which the pilgrim sons of God have sometimes to pass, after the time that they apprehend by faith what was accomplished for them on the one hill, and before they finally ascend the other. And just as the "valley" supposes the hills, so the "shadow" implies light—the light which streams from these two hills—the light of grace and the light of glory.

Let us now observe the full and ample provision that has been made for us as we journey through the valley : "Thou art with me ; Thy rod and Thy staff they comfort me ". In oriental lands the shepherd carries two instruments, namely the rod or crook, and the staff. By the former of these he guides the sheep in dangerous passes, placing the crook under their necks, one by one, and holding them up to assist their steps. The latter he uses for the defence of the sheep against the attacks of wild animals. Thus the provision is three-fold :

(1) *Companionship*—"Thou art with me ". Till now, David has been speaking *of* the Shepherd ; but as the valley of death's shade is approached he begins to speak *to* Him. Instead of saying "He" he says "*Thou* art with me ". The word of confidence which David uses here, is transmuted for us into a word of promises by our Lord. "I am with you *always*," He says (Matthew 28. 20) ; and again, "I will *never* leave thee nor forsake thee" (Hebrews 13. 5). Come dark valley or bright sunshine, green pasture or desert land—" *I am with you always* ". That is a fact, irrespective of the strength or

weakness of our faith ; apart from, and entirely independent of, what we feel.   Our feelings may change as
frequently as do the winds ; our experience of the blessedness of the promise may rise or fall as frequently as do
the tides ; but the promise and the Promiser abide.

A man once came to a preacher, and said to him : " I
was filled with joy in the meeting yesterday, and now it
has all gone—*all*—and I do not know what to do.   It is
as dark as night. "

" I am so glad," was the reply.

He looked at the servant of Christ with astonishment,
and said : " What do you mean ? "

" Yesterday, God gave you joy, and to-day He sees you
are resting on your emotions instead of on Christ, and He
has taken them away in order to turn you to Christ.
You have lost your joy, but *you have Christ none the less*.
Did you ever pass through a railway tunnel ? "

" Yes, often."

" Did you, because it was dark, become melancholy
and alarmed ? "

" Of course not."

" And did you, after a while, come out again into the
light ? "

" *I am out now*," he exlaimed, interrupting the servant
of Christ ;   " it is all right—feelings or no feelings ".

(2) *Guidance*—" Thy crook (Thy rod)".   Dr. Duff tells
how that once, while he was travelling in the Himalayas,
he saw a native shepherd, followed by his flock.   The
man frequently looked back, and, if he noticed a sheep
going too near the edge of the precipice, he would gently
draw it towards the rest by applying his crook to its hind
leg.   And so " He will keep the feet of His saints " (1
Samuel 2. 9).   " The steps of a good man are ordered by
the Lord ; and He delighteth in his way.   Though he fall
he shall not be utterly cast down ; for the Lord upholdeth
him with His hand " (see Psalm 37. 23, 24).

(3)   *Defence*—" Thy staff " (see John 10. 11-14).

Divine Companionship ; Heavenly Guidance ; Omnipotent Defence !

In conclusion, let us notice carefully that we walk not *in* the valley, but *through* it ; for there is a vast distinction between the two prepositions. A person might wander for a very long time *in*, say, West Street ; but it does not take him long, however, to walk *through* it. Is it not even so with the trials incidental to Christian life and warfare ? Our Marahs are followed by our Elims ; " the dews of sorrow are aye lustred by His love ; our web of time is woven with mercy and with judgment ". As we pass through the trial, the Word is—" When thou passest *through* the waters, I will be with thee ; and *through* the rivers they shall not overflow thee ; when thou walkest *through* the fire, thou shalt not be burned ; neither shall the flame kindle upon thee " (Isaiah 43. 2). Should the trial continue, *this* is the Word : " Who is among you that feareth the Lord, that obeyeth the voice of His servant, that walketh in darkness and hath no light ? Let him trust in the name of the Lord and stay upon his God " (Isaiah 50. 10).

And, finally, we should remember that the reason why we are allowed to pass through such an experience at all is that we might be led to the rich fields of light and plenty which lie beyond it. " We went through fire and through water ; but Thou broughtest us out into a *wealthy place* " (Psalm 66. 12).

Chapter VII

THE THREEFOLD SECRET

" I shall not want " (verse 1); " Thou art with me "
(verse 4); " For ever with the Lord " (verse 6)

THE great Beecher has said that Psalm 23 " has
charmed more griefs to rest than all the philosophy of
the world " ; and the devout Maclaren, that the reading
of it to one in trial is like " laying a handful of snow on a
fevered brow ". What has helped as much as anything
else, perhaps, to produce these blessèd results has been
the discovery of its three great secrets. It unlocks the
secret of a peaceful life—provided by the Lord (verse 1) ;
it reveals the secret of a triumphant death—companionship of the Lord (verse 4) ; and it unfolds the secret of a
glad eternity—for ever with the Lord (verse 6).

In the belief that to do so will quicken our faith,
strengthen our hope, and deepen our love for Christ, we
turn briefly to consider these.

I. THE SECRET OF A PEACEFUL LIFE : " I shall not
want "—provision *by* the Lord (verse 1). Psalm 22
represents our Lord as dying to save, and Psalm 23 as
living to provide. These two thoughts are brought
together in one New Testament Scripture—Romans 8. 32.
" He that spared not His own Son but delivered Him up
for us all "—that is Psalm 22 ; " how shall He not with
Him also freely give us all things ? "—that is Psalm 23.

The chapter which exhaustively discusses divine provision for daily needs is Matthew 6. The argument there
is that as the greater always includes the less, so He Who
has purchased the jewel will not forget the requirements
of the casket in which it dwells ; He, Who, at infinite
cost, met the needs of the soul, will not fail to supply the

needs of the body. There are, however, two dangers which, in this connection, constantly beset us, and against which we are to guard.

There is, first, the danger of desiring *too much* (Matthew 6. 19). And that the danger is a very real one is evident from the solemn language which Scripture uses in warning against it. " They that will be rich fall into temptation and a snare, and into many foolish and hurtful lusts, which drown men in destruction and perdition. For the love of money is the root of all evil : which while some coveted after, they have erred from the faith, and pierced themselves through with many sorrows " (1 Timothy 6. 9, 10). When the desire to accumulate wealth becomes the supreme passion in a Christian's heart, he ceases to have those heavenward aspirations which normally characterize the possessors of the divine life ; for where his treasure is, there his heart is also (Matthew 6. 21). Speaking of " Mammon ", Milton says that he was

> " The least erected spirit that fell from heaven ;
> For even in heaven his looks and thoughts
> Were always *downward bent*, admiring more
> The riches of heaven's pavement, trodden gold,
> That aught divine or holy else enjoyed
> In vision beatific ".

To obviate this danger, we are exhorted to be content with such things as we have (see 1 Timothy 6. 6-8 ; Hebrews 13. 5) ; and, instead of trusting in uncertain riches, to trust in the living God, Who giveth us richly all things to enjoy (1 Timothy 6. 17).

The second danger is that of fearing and worrying lest we shall *not have enough* (Matthew 6. 25). We once heard of a poor coloured woman, who earned a precarious living by daily labour, but who was a joyous, triumphant Christian. " Ah, Nancy," said a gloomy Christian lady to her one day, who almost disapproved of her constant cheerfulness, and yet envied it, " Ah, Nancy, it is all well enough to be happy now ; but I should think the thoughts of your future would sober you. Only suppose, for instance, you should have a spell of sickness, and be unable to work ; or suppose your present employers should move away, and no one else should give you anything to do ; or suppose—." " Stop ! " cried Nancy, " I never supposes. De Lord is my Shepherd, and I know I shall not want, and, honey," she added to her gloomy friend, " it's all dem *supposes* as is makin' you so mis'able. You'd better give dem all up and just trust de Lord." To dismiss " dem supposes " our Lord turns us to the little birds of the air and the flowers of the field (Matthew 6. 25-34). May we take the comfort which these great words are intended to yield us ; and endeavour to seek first the kingdom of God, knowing that " all these things " shall be added unto us (verse 33).

But there are profounder needs than those which can be met by pounds, shillings, and pence. There are the needs of the heart, the needs of the mind ; and it is in the supplying of these that Christianity shines forth in incomparable magnificence, and in inimitable grandeur. Its adaptability to human need and sorrow has been tested and proved by prince and peasant, by sage and savage, by those occupying the loftiest, as well as by those occupying the lowliest stations in life. A brilliant writer of last century once declared that it was the privilege of every Christian to have three things : he has the inexhaustible resources of God to draw upon, the moral glories of the Lord Jesus Christ to gaze upon, and the living depths of Holy Scripture to feed upon. What is that but saying, in other words, that " my God shall supply all your needs—spiritual, mental, and physical— according to His riches in glory by Christ Jesus " (Philippians 4. 19). *There* is the promise, but we must not forget to claim it ; for an unclaimed promise is just like an uncashed cheque—of no practical value.

II. THE SECRET OF A TRIUMPHANT DEATH : " Thou art with me "—companionship *of* the Lord (verse 4).

We need say little on this, for we have already seen what the New Testament says about it. Let us, however, be reminded of two Scriptures : " Lo, I am with you always, even unto the *end* " (Matthew 28. 20) ; and " absent from the body, present with the Lord " (2 Corinthians 5. 8). Death, for the Christian, is not the " king of terrors ", but simply the messenger who summons him into the more immediate presence of the King of kings. It comes, not like an officer of the law to drag the soul to an eternal prison-house, but as the gentle hand which unlatches the door of the cage, and lets the ransomed spirit fly to its native home amidst the skies. Coleridge spoke truly when he said :

> " Is that a death-bed where the Christian lies ?
> Yes, but not his, for death itself there dies ".

III. THE SECRET OF A GLAD ETERNITY: " In the House of the Lord for ever "—for ever *with* the Lord (verse 6). This we shall discuss in a subsequent chapter. Meanwhile, let us observe that when this glad hope is fulfilled we shall have reached *the time of perfect knowledge.* " Now we know in part, but then shall we know even as also we are known " (1 Corinthians 13. 12 ; John 13. 7). The tangled network of life will then be unravelled, and the dark mysteries of suffering and permitted wrong will be fully explained. We shall then, too, have reached *the place of perfect vision.* " Now we see through a glass darkly ; but then face to face." " His servants shall see His face." " We shall see Him as He is " (1 Corinthians 13. 12 ; Revelation 22. 4 ; 1 John 3. 2). And, finally, we shall have reached *the hour of perfect satisfaction.* " I shall be satisfied when I awake with Thy likeness " (Psalm 17. 15).

> " A little while, and we shall stand without,
> No more to hear His voice ; but enter in
> With joy unspeakable, to see His face."

CHAPTER VIII

FEASTED — ANOINTED — BLESSED

" Thou preparest a table before me in the presence of mine
enemies ; Thou anointest my head with oil ; my cup
runneth over " (verse 5)

THE ordinary interpretation of Psalm 23 is that it
brings before us a three-fold picture—the Shepherd
and His sheep in verse 1 ; the traveller and his Guide in
verse 4 ; and the Host and His guest in verse 5. But,
while that may be true by application, it is not the
primary significance of this portion of Scripture. From
start to finish Psalm 23 sings of shepherd life. The
" valley of the shadow of death " of which it speaks refers
to those places of deadly peril through which the flocks
have sometimes to pass, and in which they are cast
entirely on the guidance and protection of the shepherd.
This, as we have already seen, symbolizes the darker and
more difficult portions of the path over which the flock
of God travels to the heavenly land. Then, as regards
the " preparing of a table before me in the presence of
mine enemies ", it has been said by one who is familiar
with shepherd-life in oriental lands, that " there is no
higher task of the shepherd in Eastern countries than to
go from time to time to study places, and examine the
grass, and find a good and safe feeding-place for his sheep.
There are many poisonous plants in the grass, and the
shepherd must find and avoid them. Then there are
viper's holes, and the reptiles bite the noses of the sheep
if they are not driven away. And round the feeding-
place, which the shepherd thus prepares, in holes and
caves in the hill-sides, there are jackals, wolves, hyenas
and tigers ; and the bravery and skill of the shepherd are

at the highest point in closing up the dens with stones, or slaying the wild beasts with his long-bladed knife. Of nothing do you hear the shepherds boasting more proudly than of their achievements in this part of their care of their flocks."

Now, let us take up the three clauses of which our text is composed, and we shall find two key-words for each of them.

I. " Thou preparest a table before me in the presence of mine enemies "—DEPENDENCE AND INDEPENDENCE. Our " dependence " arises from the fact that we are in the presence of our enemies ; our " independence " comes from the fact that God spreads a table for us there. The New Testament teaches that the enemies of the people of God are the world (John 15. 18, 19), the flesh (Galatians 5. 17, R.V.), and the devil (1 Peter 5. 8). The world—an *external* foe ; the flesh—an *internal* foe ; the devil—an *infernal* foe. The first of these seeks to allure from the path of happy fellowship with, and service for, Christ (2 Tim. 4. 10) ; the second, to entice into sin (James 1. 14) ; while the third resists every effort of the believing soul to advance in the knowledge of God (Ephesians 6. 11). The allurements of the world are nullified by a lively apprehension of the love of the Father (1 John 2. 15) ; the flesh is opposed by the indwelling Spirit (Galatians 5. 16) ; and the devil having been annulled by Christ is now a conquered foe (see Hebrews 2. 14, 15 ; James 4. 7). Thus we have opposing us a trinity of evil which is mighty ; and we have helping us a Trinity of good which is almighty.

But if the presence of our enemies makes us absolutely dependent upon God, the table spread there renders us absolutely independent of man. Alexander the Great once asked Diogenes if he could do him any favour. " The only favour that I ask of you," said the philosopher, " is that you do not stand between me and the sun ". That is about all the Christian need ask of the world—" do

not stand between me and my Lord—the Sun of
Righteousness ". In Psalm 78. 19 the question is asked,
" Can God furnish a table in the wilderness ? " and that
question finds its most effective answer in the history of
the people who propounded it (see verses 12 to 20). The
reason why, after such displays of divine power and goodness, they asked such a question is given in verse 22—
" they believed not "—and thus it ever is. Unbelief
asks, " Can God ? " but it is the prerogative of faith to
transpose the words, and by so doing to transform the
unbelieving question into a triumphant declaration of
confidence. Instead of saying, " Can God ? " faith says,
" God can "—" Thou preparest a table before me in sight
of, and in spite of, mine enemies ". Unbelief judges God
in the presence of the difficulty ; faith judges the difficulty
in the presence of God. The former looks at the enemy
and says, " we are *not* able " (Numbers 13. 31) ; " if we
advance *we* shall be eaten up " (verse 32). The latter
fixes its gaze upon God and says, " we are *well* able "
(Numbers 13. 30) ; " if we advance we shall eat *them* up "
(Numbers 14. 9). Difficulties are only food for faith.

But with what is the wilderness table laden ? we ask.
And the answer is again given in the sixth chapter of
John—" I am the Bread of Life," said Jesus, " he that
cometh to Me shall never hunger ; and he that believeth
on Me shall never thirst " (6. 35). It is very instructive
to note that many things which are predicated of the
written Word are predicated also of the Living Word.
" Thy Word is Truth "—" I am the Truth " (compare
John 17. 17 ; 14. 6). " The words that I speak unto
you they are life "—" I am . . . the Life ". " Thy
Word is a light unto my path "—" I am the Light of the
world " (John 8. 12 ; Psalm 119. 105 and 130). And
when the written Word serves its purpose of leading us
into fellowship with the Living Word, we are then at the
secret source of every precious thing. The Christian
believer has hungerings, yearnings, and aspirations, which

this world can neither understand nor answer, which even the gifts of God cannot satisfy.

> " Thy gifts will not suffice,
> Our spirits yearn for Thee."

But Christ is enough the mind and heart to fill. He can touch the deepest springs of our nature (Matthew 5. 6) ; He can meet the profoundest wants of the soul (Psalm 107. 9).

> " Art thou hungry ?   Christ is bread (John 6. 33).
> Feed no more on husks instead.
> Thirsty ?   He is drink indeed (Psalm 42. 2).
> He can satisfy thy need.
> Christ is riches—art thou poor ?   (Eph. 3. 8).
> Come to Him and want no more."

II.   " Thou anointest my head with oil "—FRESHNESS AND FULNESS.   By comparing the Scriptures which speak of it we learn that this " anointing " produces freshness (Psalm 92. 10) ; and joy (Psalm 45. 7) ; just as its absence denotes mourning (2 Samuel 14. 2) ; and sadness (Matthew 6. 16-18).   And it is evident that Psalm 45. 7 applies primarily to the Lord Jesus, Who, though a Man of sorrows and acquainted with grief, was, nevertheless, anointed with the oil of gladness above His fellows (Isaiah 53. 3 ; Hebrews 1. 8, 9).   Holiness and happiness are as firmly linked together as are sin and sorrow.   Spotlessly holy, His joy was deep, tranquil, and perennial ; but in " bearing away the sin of the world ", He endured suffering and sorrow of which we can have no conception, but in the contemplation of which we can only worship and adore.   And because the dignity of His person adds infinite and eternal value to His redemptive work, the bitter cry which fell from His lips on the hill called Calvary, shall find its echo in the triumph-songs of the redeemed throughout eternity.

We, too, have received an anointing from the Holy One

(2 Corinthians 1. 21), which anointing abides with us (1 John 2. 27). Do we manifest the results which should flow from it—freshness and joyfulness? It is solemnly possible, by careless indifference, as well as by committing actual sin, so to grieve the Spirit of God as to nullify the effects of this sacred anointing. Instead of engaging the soul with the exalted Christ, which is the normal work of the Spirit (John 16. 13-15), He will then have to occupy us with our failure, which means that celestial light has to be exchanged for mournful gloom, and the peace of God for the unrest of sin. When, however, the Spirit is unhindered and ungrieved, self is forgotten; and He Whose redemptive work is to form the subject of eternal song, becomes Himself the object of the soul's gaze now. And with what result? Why, that " we all with unveiled face beholding as in a mirror the glory of the Lord, are transformed into the same image from glory to glory, even as by the Spirit of the Lord " (2 Corinthians 3. 18).

But there is not only freshness, there is also fulness; and connected with that is the thought of power. We read of the Lord Jesus that " He was anointed with the Holy Ghost and with power " (Acts 10. 38); and what was true of Him may be true of us (John 3. 34, R.V.; Luke 11. 13). Besides these Scriptures there is the definite, positive command, " Be filled with the Spirit " (Ephesians 5. 18). It is well to remember in this connection that *ordinarily* the Spirit of God works by and through the Word of God. However blissful our experiences, however ecstatic our visions, unless there is a deep and real work of the Word of God in heart and life the visions will fade, the bliss will prove evanescent, and will leave the soul a prey to the evil one. And, as was the case with Bunyan's pilgrims the probability is that we shall be led into Bye-path Meadow, thence to Doubting Castle, and finally into the hands of Giant Despair. In Ephesians 5. 18 we have the command " be filled with the Spirit ", with certain results predicted. In Colossians

3. 16, we have the exhortation " let the Word of Christ dwell in you richly ", with certain results predicted. If we compare these results we shall find them to be identical. If it be a true proposition which declares that " two causes which produce the same effect are equal ", then we can at once see how closely associated with the Word of God is the work of the Spirit of God. To have the Word without the Spirit is equal to having rails laid, and the locomotive thereon, but without any power to propel it. To have the Spirit without the Word, is to have the power which propels, but no rails to guide. To have both Word and Spirit is to have guidance and power, and ensures the full enjoyment in the life, of all that is suggested by the " anointing "—freshness and fulness, joy and power.

III. " My cup runneth over "—BLESSED AND BLESS-ING. The cup of judgment was drained for us by our Lord (Matthew 26. 42) ; the cup of salvation He has mixed for us out of the chalice of His supreme sufferings (Psalm 116. 13) ; and now the cup of blessing overflows from us to others (Psalm 23. 5). This is ever the divine order : we must be vessels of mercy ere we can be channels of blessing ; the " well " of living water meeting all local requirements must precede the " rivers " which are to flow out in blessing to others (compare John 4. 14 and John 7. 37, 38).

" My cup runneth over." What does that mean ? Abundance ? It means more than that ; it means redundance. How does a vessel overflow ? Only by being under, and as long as it is kept under, a flowing fountain. He is the fountain of living water (see Jeremiah 2. 13) ; and if we are in touch with Him there is no limit to what He can accomplish in, and by, and with, and for, and through us. Then, indeed, shall we be like Abraham of old—blessed and made a blessing (Genesis 12. 2).

" Thou in the presence of an envious foe,
My banquet spreading, pouring on my brow
Anointing oil—and lo ! my flowing cup
In copious streams Thy bounty's gift declares.
Thus, even thus, through all my days of life,
I feel Thee ever near ; Thy mercy's grace,
The blessings of Thy love, my course attend,
Oh, where but in Thy temple, in what home,
Save in the dwelling of his Lord and God !
For evermore shall David fix his rest."

CHAPTER IX

GOODNESS AND MERCY

" Surely goodness and mercy shall follow me all the days
of my life " (verse 6)

BEFORE looking at what these words suggest it may
be helpful to recapitulate what has been before us in
our study of this—" The Pearl of Psalms ". This can be
best done, perhaps, by observing what has been called its
seven-fold positions. Psalm 23 represents us as occupying successively seven distinct positions : (1) underneath
us—green pastures ; (2) beside us—still waters ; (3) with
us—the Lord ; (4) before us—a table prepared ; (5)
around us—enemies ; (6) behind us—goodness and
mercy ; (7) above us—the House of the Lord. Thus, if
the retrospective glance calls forth gratitude and thank-
fulness, the prospective glance imparts joyfulness and
confidence.

> " We praise Him for all that is past,
> And trust Him for all that's to come."

We shall consider in this chapter, the sixth of these
positions ; and, in the next and closing chapter, the
seventh.

" Surely GOODNESS and MERCY shall follow me all the
days of my life." It would be difficult to find two other
words to describe as accurately as do the two great words
of our text, the two-fold provision which has been made
by our God for believers of New Testament times. " Goodness "—that is for our *need*, and corresponds to what the
priesthood of Christ provides (see Heb. 4. 14-16) ;
" Mercy "—that is for our *failure*, and well describes what
is secured for us by the advocacy of Christ (1 John 2. 1).

I. GOODNESS. In Hebrews 9. 24-28 there are three "appearings" of Christ spoken of. He *hath* appeared—as a Sacrifice (verse 26) ; He *now* appears—as a Priest (verse 24) ; He *shall* appear—as a Saviour (verse 28). At the present moment, therefore, He now appears in the presence of God for us (verse 24) ; and, seeing He ever liveth there to make intercession for us (7. 25), we are enjoined to "come boldly unto the throne of grace, that we may obtain mercy, and find grace to help in time of need " (4. 14-16).

David, in common with ourselves, knew what it was to grow weary in the fight : "I had fainted," he says, "unless I had believed to see the *goodness* of the Lord in the land of the living " (Psalm 27. 13) ; and his counsel in this connection strongly resembles that of the writer to the Hebrews. " Wait on the Lord and He shall strengthen thine heart," says the former ; " come boldly to the throne of grace that we may find help in time of need," says the latter (compare Psalm 27. 14 ; Hebrews 4. 16).

The value of what is secured for us by the priesthood of Christ may be learned from that which, in the Levitical economy, foreshadowed it. It will be recalled that the names of the children of Israel were engraven on two onyx stones, that these two stones were placed upon the shoulders of the ephod, and that Aaron the high priest thus bore those names *upon his shoulders* before the Lord (see Exodus 28. 9-14). They also appeared on the breastplate, as we learn from Exodus 28. 15-29, " And Aaron shall bear the names of the children of Israel in the breastplate *upon his heart* when he goeth into the Holy Place, for a memorial before the Lord continually " (verse 29). Now, the " heart " is spoken of as the place of affection, and " shoulders " as the place of strength ; and the beautiful suggestion is that the high priest's strength and affection, his power and his love, were engaged on behalf of those whom he represented before God. And when we

think of Him Who is our great High Priest, we remember
with gratitude that

> " The atoning work is done,
> The precious blood is shed,
> And Jesus now has gone
> His people's cause to plead.
> He lives in heaven—their great High Priest—
> And bears their names upon His breast ".

We remember also that, in virtue of that fact, He can
meet our profoundest needs ; He can sympathize ; He
can succour ; He can sustain.   He can *sympathize*—
because, being Man as well as God, He " was in all points
tempted like as we are, yet without sin ", and is now
" touched with the feeling of our infirmities " (Hebrews
4. 15).   He can *succour*—because, being God as well as
Man, all power in heaven and on earth is committed to
Him (Matthew 28. 18).   He can *sustain*—because, since He
ever lives to intercede, He can save completely all that
draw near unto God through Him (Hebrews 7. 25, R.V.).
And, sorrowing one, in thy hour of grief and of brokenness,
remember that the goodness of God follows thee—provid-
ing thee a great High Priest, Who, by the exquisite sym-
pathy of His exalted human nature, can interpret and
can meet, as none other can, the most trying needs of
thy life.

   II.   MERCY.   But suppose we fail to avail ourselves of
the high-priestly provision which has been made for us—
what happens then ?   Does He cast us off for ever ?
That is what we would deserve, no doubt ; but that is not
what He does.   Writing to Christians, the apostle John
says, " if any man sin, we have an Advocate with the
Father, Jesus Christ the righteous " (1 John 2. 1).   And
the basis of that advocacy is given in the next verse—
" He is the propitiation for our sins " (verse 2).

   " Ah," says the sceptic, " just what I told you—
Christianity is simply ' a means of escape ' ".   But is it ?
We may safely affirm that the man who reasons so under-

stands neither the grace of God nor the holiness of God.
When Christ comes to a man He comes with blessings in
both hands : in one hand He holds out salvation, forgive-
ness, eternal life ; in the other He holds out holiness of
life, righteousness of character ; and the man who pro-
fesses to accept the former and yet absolutely disregards
the latter is, in all probability, deceiving himself. To a
poor sinning woman who was brought by a number of
hypocrites to the Master for judgment, this was His
gracious word : " Neither do I condemn thee ; *go and sin
no more* ". There we have the blessing in both hands !
(John 8. 11). The sovereign grace which is displayed in
the first part of that statement is only equalled by the
holiness of life which is imperatively demanded in the
second. Legalism would transpose these parts, and
antinomianism would separate them ; but they admit
neither of transposition nor of separation ; and, taken
as they stand, they illustrate the provisions of the gospel,
and the requirements of the gospel.

But in connection with the advocacy of Christ, let us
specially mark the word " if "—" *If* any man sin, we
have an Advocate with the Father " for this word is
the key to the understanding of our theme. The grace
that makes a man a Christian leaves him still *a man*. He
is not impeccable ; for he still has a deceitful heart and a
tempting devil to contend with. Hence the force of the
word " *if* any man sin "—the possibility of sinning is
admitted, but its necessity denied. When a Christian
does sin, however, he is dealt with not penally but pater-
nally ; not as a convict, but as a son. When our little
son disobeys us, we do not send him to the police station
to be dealt with, do we ? The relationship which we
bear to him gives us the right, and lays upon us the
responsibility, to deal with him ourselves. And so, if a
believer sins (i.e., practises sin) his Heavenly Father will
judge him (see 1 Peter 1. 17) ; he will be chastened by the
Lord that he may not be condemned with the world (1

Corinthians 11. 32). It is impossible for God to treat sin lightly ; and His disciplinary chastisement of His people, who give way to it, will eventually make it impossible for any of them to regard it lightly either. But, should we be tripped in an unwatchful moment, let us remember the word : " if any man sin, we have an Advocate with the Father, Jesus Christ the righteous ". Satan may " accuse " (Revelation 12. 10), but he cannot " condemn " (Romans 8. 33, 34) ; the propitiatory sacrifice of our blessèd Lord shall retain its efficacy " till every ransomed saint of God be saved to sin no more " (1 John 1. 7). Whole-hearted confession—which embraces self-judgment and the abhorring and forsaking of that which interrupted communion—is the divinely-appointed method of bringing us once again into the enjoyment of that which the advocacy of Christ secures (1 John 1. 9).

Thus " goodness " is manifested in the provision of One Who ever lives to intercede ; while " mercy " follows us to remove entirely all traces of those sad footprints which we make when, through unwatchfulness, we go astray.

A servant of the Lord once asked an artist if he could paint a picture of an Eastern shepherd, and the artist replied that he could. " And can you paint the sheep which follow the shepherd ? " " Yes, I can." " And can you paint the goodness and mercy which follow the sheep ? " was the next query ; to which the artist had to reply that that was quite beyond him. It reminds one of the aged Christian, who, after fifty years' experience of the goodness of God, said that if she had raised a stone of remembrance every time the Lord had helped her (1 Samuel 7. 12), she would have built a solid wall fifty years in length.

CHAPTER X

THE DESIRED HAVEN

" I will dwell in the House of the Lord for ever "
(verse 6)

BLESSÈD conclusion to a blessèd theme ! Dark valleys may require to be traversed (verse 4) ; malignant foes may have to be encountered (verse 5) ; but beyond the former, and in a scene where the latter can never enter—a realm where all is harmony, and light, and love—we shall live eternally—" I will dwell in the House of the Lord for ever ".

But these words do not wholly apply to the future : there is a very real sense in which they may be true now. Not only shall we dwell in " the House of the Lord " for *all eternity* ; we may do so for *all time*.

I.   FOR ALL ETERNITY.   In the clear light of the New Testament we can assert that every child of God will infallibly dwell in the House of the Lord for all eternity. " In My Father's House," said the Lord Jesus, " are many mansions . . . I go to prepare a place for you " (John 14. 2).   And, after He accomplished redemption, we find Him linking us with Himself in the unspeakably blessèd relationship which this verse sets forth :   " I ascend unto My Father and your Father " (John 20. 17 ; Galatians 3. 26).   " And if I go," He continues, " I will come again and receive you unto Myself, that where I am there ye may be also " (John 14. 3).   This is confirmed in 1 Thessalonians 4. 13-18, where the apostle, describing the events which will take place at the second coming of our Lord, declares that we " shall be caught up to meet the Lord in the air ; and so shall we ever be with the Lord ".   What a strong and sure hope ; what a grand

and glorious destiny ! The hope is strong and sure because the anchor will never drag (Hebrews 6. 19) ; and the cable will never snap (John 10. 35) ; and the destiny is grand and glorious because when He shall appear we shall be like Him, for we shall see Him as He is (1 John 3. 2). Then HE shall be satisfied, for He shall see of the travail of His soul (Isaiah 53. 11) ; and then WE shall be satisfied, for we shall awake with His likeness (Psalm 17. 15).

> " He and I, in that bright glory,
> One deep joy shall share,
> Mine to be for ever with Him,
> His that I am there."

II. FOR ALL TIME. " Ah," we sigh, " all *that* lies in the future, and we believe every word of it ; but what about the present ? Have these words no message for us *now* ?" Most assuredly they have. We may antedate their literal fulfilment by experiencing, even down here in the midst of the toil, the sorrow, and the heartache, " days of heaven upon earth " (Deuteronomy 11. 21). In Psalm 23. 6 David says : " I shall dwell in the House of the Lord *for ever* " ; and in Psalm 27. 4 he says, " One thing have I desired of the Lord, that will I seek after ; that I may dwell in the House of the Lord *all the days of my life*, to behold the beauty of the Lord and to enquire in His temple ". And referring once again to the fourteenth chapter of John, we find that which answers to these two aspects of this great truth. In verse 2, Jesus says, " In My Father's House are many mansions " ; and in verse 23, " If a man love Me, he will keep My words : and My Father will love him, and We will come unto him and make Our abode with him " (same Greek word as in verse 2). And thus we see that, while faith brings the soul to Heaven, faith and implicit obedience bring heaven into the soul.

In Psalm 27. 4, David gives two reasons for this desire, the first of these being that he might " behold the beauty

of the Lord ". And since it is the law of influence that
we become like that which we habitually admire, he
simply anticipates the profound statement of the inspired
apostle who declared that " we all, with unveiled face,
beholding as in a mirror the glory of the Lord, are transformed into the same image from glory to glory, even as
by the Spirit of the Lord " (2 Corinthians 3. 18).

> " The soul whose sight all-quickening grace renews,
> Takes the resemblance of the One she views,
> As diamonds stripped of their opaque disguise,
> Reflect the noon-tide glory of the skies."

It is instructive to note that the word which in 2 Corinthians 3. 18 (R.V.), is translated " transformed " occurs
only three times in the New Testament. It occurs in
Matthew 17. 2, where, speaking of what transpired on the
Mount of Transfiguration, we are told that our Lord
" was *transfigured* before them ". It occurs again in
Romans 12. 2, where we have the exhortation, " be ye
transformed by the renewing of your mind ". And it
occurs for the third time in 2 Cor. 3. 18. The first of
these Scriptures shows the pattern *to* which, the second
reveals the principle *upon* which, and the third supplies
the power *by* which, we are to be transformed.

There is the principle of true holiness—heart occupation
with the exalted Christ. Communion with Him is the
one infallible method of excommunicating sin. It is at
once the safest and most effective restraint from vice ; the
surest and most powerful incentive to virtue.

Dannecker, the German sculptor, spent eight years in
producing a face of Christ, and at last wrought out one
in which the emotions of love and sorrow were so blended
that beholders wept as they looked upon it. Subse-
quently, being solicited to employ his great talent on the
statue of Venus, he replied, " After gazing so long into the
face of Christ, think you that I can now turn my attention
to a heathen goddess ? " That is the secret ; and those
who learn it will be able to say with Ephraim : " I have

heard Him, and observed Him ; what have I to do any more with idols ? " (Hosea 14. 8).

The second reason which David gives for desiring to dwell in the House of the Lord is that he might " enquire in His temple ". Shakespeare tells us that there are more things in heaven and earth than are dreamt of in the philosophies ; and since the simple-hearted child of God can see further on his knees than the eagled-eyed philosopher can on his tip-toes, our truest wisdom lies in bringing our questionings, and the problems which ever and anon present themselves to every thoughtful mind, to the One Who alone can give the answer. As we look around, we see that " right " is frequently on the scaffold, and " wrong " is as frequently on the throne ; like the Psalmist we behold the wicked prospering (Psalm 73. 3-9), and the righteous suffering (verse 10) ; and as we ourselves constantly come face to face with this ever baffling problem, we are driven to ask—" Doth God know ? Is there knowledge in the Most High ? " (verse 11). Like him, however, we shall find the explanation to this perplexing mystery only by going " into the sanctuary of God " (verses 16-28), and by " enquiring in His temple " (Psalm 27. 4).

Without pursuing this theme, we would say that to obtain a divine explanation of two of the greatest of life's mysteries—the mystery of suffering, and the apparent triumph of evil over good—we cannot do better than reverently ponder such portions of God's Word as the Book of Job, the twelfth chapter of Hebrews and Psalms 37 and 73. " Suffering finds its philosophy not in organic penalty and retributive judgment only, but also in disciplinary chastisement and educative development."

> " The ills we see—
> The mysteries of suffering deep and long,
> The dark enigmas of permitted wrong—
>   Have all one key ;
> This strange, sad world is but our Father's school ;
> All chance and change His love shall grandly overrule."

It is easy to write about these things (i.e., " beholding
the beauty of the Lord " and " enquiring in His temple"),
and easier still to read about them ; but where are we in
regard to the practical enjoyment of them ?   Can we say
with the writer of this Psalm that we *desire* them and *seek*
after them ? (Psalm 27. 4).   It will not do merely to
desire them ; for " the soul of the sluggard desireth and
hath nothing " (Proverbs 13. 4).   There must be purpose
of heart, steadfast exercise of will, energy of soul (Acts
11. 23).   " If . . . thou shalt seek the Lord, thou shalt
find Him, if thou seek Him with all thy heart and with all
thy soul " (Deuteronomy 4. 29).   " Blessèd are they that
keep His testimonies and that seek Him with the whole
heart " (Psalm 119. 2).   Speaking of her experience of
the blessedness which flows from this concentration of
purpose in seeking the face of God, Frances Ridley
Havergal—one of the saintliest of women, and sweetest of
poetesses—says :

> " I never thought it could be thus—
>   Month after month to know
> The river of Thy peace, without
>   One ripple in its flow :
> Without one quiver in the trust,
>   One flicker in its glow ".

There are two things which characterize a man of the
world, namely, his home and his business.   But the order
is, *from* his home *to* his business ; and if his home be a
happy one, he carries the fragrance of it with him to his
business.   Exactly so is it with the Christian ; his
" home " is in Heaven, his " business " is to work for
Christ on earth.

We once heard a preacher say of Dr. Bonar that, as one
beheld him in the pulpit, and heard him preach, the
impression created was that the Doctor had just come
from the presence of God for a few moments to deliver a
message, and that he intended to go back there immediately after he had delivered it.   The time is approach--

ing, however, when we shall go " no more out ", which, by the way, is one of the many differences between Eden and Heaven—the final Home of the redeemed. The former had a way out, but not a way in ; the latter has a way in, but happily has no way out.

Fellow-pilgrim to the realms of endless glory, let us look upwards and onwards—" the coming of the Lord draweth nigh ". Let us lay aside every weight ; let us forget those things which are behind—the weaknesses and the waverings, the failures and the follies ; and let us run with patience the race that is set before us, looking for that blessèd hope and the glorious appearing of the great God and our Saviour Jesus Christ.

> " A little while, the desert will be o'er,
> The head shall ache, the heart shall grieve no more ;
> Our golden harps before the throne shall raise
> Our ever-new, eternal song of praise.
> In hope we lift our wistful, longing eyes,
> Waiting to see the Morning-Star arise ;
> How bright, how glorious will His advent be,
> Th'unclouded Sun in all its majesty.
> How shall our eyes to see His face delight,
> Whose love has cheered us through the darksome night ;
> How shall our ears drink in His well-known voice,
> Whose faintest whispers make our souls rejoice !
> No stain within ; no foes or snares around ;
> No jarring notes shall there discordant sound ;
> All pure without, all pure within the breast ;
> No thorns to wound, no toil to mar our rest.
> If here on earth the thoughts of Jesu's love
> Lift our poor hearts this weary world above ;
> If even here the taste of heavenly springs
> So cheers the spirit, that the pilgrim sings :
> What will the sunshine of His glory prove ?
> What the unmingled fulness of His love ?
> What hallelujahs will His presence raise !
> What but one loud eternal burst of praise ! "